A
Columbia College Student
IN THE
Eighteenth Century

Daniel D. Tompkins

A
Columbia College Student
IN THE
Eighteenth Century

ESSAYS BY

DANIEL D. TOMPKINS
CLASS OF 1795
SOMETIME GOVERNOR OF NEW YORK STATE
AND VICE PRESIDENT OF THE
UNITED STATES

With a Foreword by
NICHOLAS MURRAY BUTLER

Edited by
RAY W. IRWIN & EDNA L. JACOBSEN

KENNIKAT PRESS, INC./PORT WASHINGTON, N. Y.

A COLUMBIA COLLEGE STUDENT IN THE EIGHTEENTH CENTURY

Copyright 1940 Columbia University Press
This edition published in 1964 by KENNIKAT PRESS

Library of Congress Catalog Card No: 64-15544

Manufactured in the United States of America

FOREWORD

THESE boyhood essays by Daniel D. Tompkins of the Class of 1795 in old Columbia College are a most admirable and unusual revelation of student interests and student opinion in the Columbia College of a century and a half ago. Tompkins lived a short life, measured by years, for he died when he was but fifty-one years of age. Nevertheless, in that short time he had been Justice of the Supreme Court of the State of New York, Chancellor of the University of the State of New York, Governor of the State of New York for ten years and Vice President of the United States for eight years. He had been a constant and most effective worker in the task of building the new nation on the foundations which the Fathers had laid for it.

That Daniel D. Tompkins is not well remembered or adequately esteemed by his countrymen of this day and generation is all too obvious. It may well be that the publication of these essays written by him in undergraduate days will do much to restore him to the place which he should occupy in the public mind.

These essays are not only admirable and cultivated in their style, but quite exceptional in the subjects with which they deal. They come from the pen of a youth who was plainly being trained in the art of reflection and of understanding. He was forming the habit of looking beneath the surface of things, however attractive and however interesting that surface might appear to be. He had a mind which was not narrow, nor was it closed to new ideas. In other words, he was a youth receiving a truly liberal education and responding to its appeal.

Outstanding is his valedictory oration, delivered on Commencement Day, May 6, 1795. There have been many Commencement Day addresses since that day, delivered by students about to be graduated, many of whom became men of large importance and high reputation. It may well be doubted whether any one of these reaches the high plane of excellence of that delivered by Tompkins. Its literary style, its charm of expression, its subject matter and its form—all unite to make it a truly noteworthy outgiving. Its closing words may well serve in these much later days to inspire and to guide, not only our youth, but their elders as well. Obviously, little old Columbia College was giving a truly liberal education as the eighteenth century, with all its profoundly interesting and important happenings, was drawing to its close.

NICHOLAS MURRAY BUTLER

Columbia University
in the
City of New York

November 1, 1940

CONTENTS

ILLUSTRATIONS

[ix]

INTRODUCTION

By Ray W. Irwin and Edna L. Jacobsen

ON THE Federal Building, Ithaca, New York, there is a tablet bearing the following inscription in honor of the man who as a lad at Columbia College wrote the essays reproduced in this volume:

IN GRATEFUL MEMORY OF

1774   DANIEL D. TOMPKINS   1825

AFTER WHOM THIS COUNTY CREATED IN 1817 IS NAMED
JUDGE OF THE NEW YORK SUPREME COURT 1804-1807
CHANCELLOR OF UNIVERSITY OF STATE OF NEW YORK
GOVERNOR OF THE STATE OF NEW YORK 1807-1817
DEFENDER OF THE FRONTIER. COMMANDER OF THE
THIRD MILITARY DISTRICT 1814-1815. WROTE HIS
MESSAGE ON ABOLITION OF SLAVERY IN NEW YORK 1817
VICE PRESIDENT OF THE UNITED STATE[S] 1817-1825
A PATRIOT OF BRILLIANT ABILITIES AND UNTIRING ENERGY
THE PEOPLE OF TOMPKINS
COUNTY ERECT THIS MEMORIAL
MAY 30, 1910[1]

This compressed but eloquent recital of the more outstanding public activities of Governor Tompkins during a trying period in American history may well raise the question as to why such a once nationally prominent figure is so little known today, even by

---

[1] Quoted from American Scenic and Historic Preservation Society, *25th Annual Report* (1920), p. 285.

professional historians. While no definitive answer to that question can be attempted here—so numerous and complex have been the circumstances tending to relegate the Governor to comparative and unmerited obscurity—we cannot omit mention of one largely contributing factor which has a real connection with the following essays.

In 1884 the New York Legislature passed and Governor Grover Cleveland approved a bill authorizing the purchase of the official correspondence of Governor Tompkins from his heirs for the sum of $5,000.[2] By this purchase the state acquired a splendid manuscript collection, consisting of official copies of letters written by him as governor and as vice-president during the years 1807-25, originals and copies of thousands of letters which he received during that period, and a large body of miscellaneous papers, a portion of which relate to the Governor's career prior to 1807. The collection embraced an enormous quantity of data pertaining to the history of New York, particularly to the role which that state played in the stirring events leading up to and including the War of 1812. Eventually the state published in three volumes[3] the letters and a few other papers written by the Governor. The

---

[2] Henry Augustus Homes, "On the Correspondence of Gov. D. D. Tompkins (1808-1824), Lately Acquired by the State, with Some Notes on His Life," in The Albany Institute, *Transactions,* XI (1888), 223-40.

[3] *Public Papers of Daniel D. Tompkins, Governor of New York, 1807-1817: Military;* with an Introduction by Hugh Hastings, State Historian, 3 vols., N. Y. and Albany, 1898-1902.

remaining manuscripts, including letters from many of the most prominent men in the United States and dealing with a very wide range of subjects, were still unpublished when the great fire of 1911 in the Capitol destroyed some of the manuscripts and badly damaged most of those which survived. After this disaster the charred remnants were assembled in many packages, placed in boxes incorrectly labeled "Provincial Papers," and until recently seem to have remained untouched.

While searching through the Manuscripts Section of the New York State Library at Albany for materials to be used in a projected biography of Governor Tompkins,[4] the editors fortunately uncovered among the remains of the Governor's unpublished papers twenty-six of his college essays, including his valedictory oration. That there were other compositions of this type in the collection purchased by the state seems quite likely. It is known that one essay, which was probably destroyed in the fire, bore the date September 15, 1792, and was entitled "On the Necessity of Establishing When Young a Character Which We Intend to Support in After Life and Act Always Agreeably Thereto."[5]

For a variety of reasons the less-damaged essays have seemed worthy of publication. Written almost a century and a half ago and in accordance with rhetorical

---

[4] In preparation by Ray W. Irwin.

[5] Referred to by John Buckley Pine in his article "Daniel D. Tompkins, Class of 1795," *Columbia University Quarterly,* IX (Dec., 1906), 2.

standards approved by many academic institutions of that day, they provide a comparatively rare example of eighteenth-century collegiate English composition. They illustrate, too, certain abiding (if not always pleasant) experiences of many generations of college students; and with perhaps a reasonable degree of fidelity they reveal the thought patterns of the youth who would later play a conspicuous part in state and national affairs. To many of the opinions which he expressed in these early writings Tompkins clung throughout his life—particularly, and perhaps most notably, those regarding slavery, capital punishment, and the diffusion of knowledge among the masses. On the other hand, his opposition to a college curriculum prominently featuring the study of Greek and Latin seems to have decreased in later years as he became more fully aware of the advantages which such a course of study afforded to persons aspiring to enter certain professions. That he eventually placed a high estimate upon the value of his own training in Greek and Latin he strongly implied in a letter which he, while Governor, wrote advising a friend to send his son to college because the latter's "want of a more thorough classical education" would "forever, keep him in the lowest and most contemptible grade of his profession."[6]

---

[6] *Public Papers of Daniel D. Tompkins: Military*, II, 494-96. Tompkins to John Grigg, Feb. 22, 1812. While urging that this friend's son continue his studies, the Governor wrote: "Mention me affectionately to master John; tell him

Of Tompkins's background and early training a few
words must here suffice. He was born June 21, 1774,
on a farm in Fox Meadow (now Scarsdale), Westchester County, New York, and was the seventh son of
Jonathan G. and Sarah (Hyatt) Tompkins. During
the early part of the American Revolution Mrs. Tompkins and her children were forced to seek safety out-
side Fox Meadow community, to which they did not
return until the end of hostilities. Meanwhile Daniel's
father, a stanch Whig, was actively engaged in military and political affairs. He became quite prominent
in state politics, his political activities eventually em-
bracing many years of distinguished service as a mem-

---

from me that he must not becloud his promising beginning
by relaxing in industry & and progress in study. I remember
when I was about his age, my vanity often induced me to
suppose that I had obtained sufficient education and information to make my way through the world with reputation and
usefulness, but my good father & and my teachers thought
otherwise & and their opinion prevailed. I have often thought
of the deplorable consequences which would have followed,
had I been allowed to follow the suggestions of my own immature judgment. This information will not perhaps be
needed by master John, who doubtless thinks more justly on
those subjects than I did, and who would not for any consideration be debarred from the privilege of continuing his
studies until he shall arrive at the age of twenty one. . . . If,
therefore, he should even speak of leaving academical studies
until he shall be advanced to the age of eighteen or twenty
years, earnestly caution him against it, for if he do leave his
studies before that age and enter into profession of a Clergyman, Lawyer or Doctor, the want of a more thorough classical education will, forever, keep him in the lowest and most
contemptible grade of his profession."

ber of the state legislature, as well as the holding of numerous other public offices. Although he never became a wealthy man, he succeeded in acquiring sufficient means to support his wife and twelve children[7] comfortably and to provide exceptional educational opportunities for his son Daniel. The latter's formal schooling prior to his entering Columbia College in 1792 consisted mainly of a year's study in a preparatory school maintained by Malcolm Campbell in New York City, followed by several years spent at the Academy of North Salem, Westchester County. It may have been during this early period (1786-91) that the lad began to use the middle initial "D."—perhaps to distinguish his name from that of some fellow student.[8]

There is every reason to conclude that at Columbia College Tompkins was an attractive and popular student. He was of medium height, blond, blue-eyed, and handsome—and with these physical attributes he combined ambition and energy, superior intelligence, an unaffected liking for people, and a remarkable fac-

---

[7] This number is given by the Albany *Argus* (January 23, 1816), and the New York *Daily Tribune* (June 19, 1910) contains the following statement: "He [Daniel] was the seventh son and the ninth child of his parents, who had three children younger than Daniel."

[8] The significance of the initial is discussed in the New York State Historical Association, *Quarterly Journal*, ·I (1919-20), 72; R. Bolton, *History of Westchester County* (New York, 1881), II, 233; and Hugh Hastings, *Daniel D. Tompkins; an Address before the Westchester County Historical Society, October 8th, 1898*, Albany, 1900, p. 4.

ulty for remembering the names and faces of persons with whom he came in contact. It seems unquestionable that by the time of his graduation this "Farmer's Boy," as he was affectionately called, gave splendid promise of becoming a popular leader in public life.[9]

---

[9] Descriptions of Tompkins have been given in DeAlva Stanwood Alexander, *Political History of the State of New York* (New York, 1906-23), I, 160; and *Public Papers of Daniel D. Tompkins: Military*, I, 9-10.

On CHOOSING PUBLIC OFFICIAL

This essay is in part illegible, having been badly dan
aged by fire. Enough of the opening sentences
legible, however, to indicate that the author is urgin
the selection of those persons who possess

. . . Wisdom virtue, honesty and a devotion to th
liberties of mankind; because it is obvious that powe
[should not] be put into the possession of a weal
man . . . [or] . . . of a bad man. . . .[1]

As in all professions habit and practice are necessary
to make a [good] performer so when a man becomes
acquainted with the functions of an [office] he is cal·
culated to act with more becoming dignity and to
cause justice to be equitably administered, inasmuch as
he becomes acquainted [with] the foibles, with the
characters of men who are most convers[ant] in that

---

[1] D. D. Tompkins Papers (Manuscripts and History Section, N. Y. State Library, Albany, N. Y.). All the Tompkins
essays reproduced here are to be found in this collection of
manuscripts; the first seven in Box 10, pkg. 2; the eighth to
the twenty-fifth in Box 6, pkg. 2; and the "Valedictory Oration" in Box 10, pkg. 3. The editors have used brackets in
the text where there has been substantial basis for a conjec-
tural reading. Where the manuscript has been too badly damaged to admit of this procedure, illegible portions have been
indicated by a series of dots. Italic passages preceding the
essays are also supplied by the editors.

line of business and is thereby calculated to choose such subordinate officers as may be fitted to discharge their duties properly [to] the general good.

Among many objections that have been made against the [eleva]tion of any man (whatever character he may support) to an important station, the principal one seems to be that by being acqua[inted] with the necessities and exigences of the people the officer has it in his power to take improper advantage of them. Is it not from the same circumstance evident that he has it also in his power to re[nder] . . . them the more essential [service?] . . .

The only criterion I know of by which to judge of the expediency of electing a man that has filled a station is to inspect into his former conduct. Has his aim hitherto been the good of the people? We may then reason from analogy that such will be his conduct hereafter. In fine so long as the people hold in their hands the chastening rod, the freedom of frequent elections [and] the right of making a change, we need not fear but that the officer will endeavor to secure the happiness and liberty of his constituents.[2]

Columbia College, June 29, 1792.

[2] The thought expressed in the closing sentence had found wide acceptance in America during and following the Revolution. In its more extreme form it was stated thus: "Where annual elections end, tyranny begins."

On THE INDIANS and

SLAVERY

The opening lines, while in part illegible, refer to opportunities which America has had

. . . to extend the Kingdom of God over those various savage nations with which she is surrounded. . . . Happy had it been for America if being warned of the calamities of war she had desisted from it when she had once obtained a glorious peace. But instead of what one would naturally expect that she would be employed in advancing the interest of her God by civilizing her neighbors the savages of the West, she has proclaimed an unnatural war against them.[3] If the funds which have been raised to support a standing army had been appropriated to the use of pious missionaries who might civilize them and spread the english language among them what pleasing hopes might we not have had from so powerful and beneficial an ally. Thus might we have explored those western countries to the advantage of mankind by being at peace and in alliance with those tribes. Thus might the life of many a native of America have been appropri-

---

[3] The allusion to an "unnatural war" against the Indians refers to the campaigns conducted south of Lake Erie by General Arthur St. Clair and, later, by General Anthony Wayne. The contest culminated in the victory of Wayne's forces at the "Battle of the Fallen Timbers" (1794) and the negotiating of the Treaty of Greenville (1795).

ated to cultivating the soil instead of idly traversing the wilderness. Thus too [might] the lives of many of our western brethren have been preserved. . . .

There are perhaps but two particulars in which the Americans are culpable and these are not civilizing the Indians and Africans. The former they are at war with and the latter are retained in ignorance and bondage. Ought not Americans to remember that he who crowned their labors with success did it that they might be free and will not *O! gratitude will not* every tender mind shudder at the awful charge against Americans of retaining in ignorance the unhappy Africans. Should not the pure blood of American patriots recoil at these actions and reform by civilizing the Indians and freeing and civilizing the Africans.[4] America will then be unparalleled. Then might we with propriety predict that "the glory of America will travel with the sun and expire with the stars."

Columbia College, August 25, 1792.

---

[4] Tompkins, like Thomas Jefferson, Patrick Henry, and many other Americans of that period, recognized the inconsistency of those slaveholders who had employed the philosophy of natural rights to justify the American Revolution. See an elaboration of Tompkins's views on this point in his other essays "On Slavery," June 22 and 28, 1793.

On THE STUDY OF THE DEAD
LANGUAGES

. . . The first study to which students are generally
directed at their admission into academies is the study
of those [dead languages]. In this study at least three
years of the most valuable part of the scholar's life is
spent,[5] in laying a foundation for his Educa[tion] by
the knowledge of Words instead of ideas. Habit has a
great influence upon youth, and in this first three years
of their study they are habituated to trust entirely to
their memories—indeed the nature of the study requires only memory instead of a good understanding;
afterwards when it is necessary that their attention
should be bestowed on studies where more exertion of
the reasoning faculties is required such as Mathematics
—then it is that their memories are not of that great
advantage to them and they are apt to conclude that
as the means by which they prospered in the study of
the dead languages fails them in the study of Mathe-

---

[5] At the time Tompkins entered Columbia College as a
sophomore, in 1792, that institution listed the Greek and
Latin prerequisites of students seeking admission to the college as follows: ability "to render into English Caesar's Com-
mentaries of the Gallic War; the Four Orations of Cicero
against Cataline; the first four Books of Virgil's Aeneid; and
the Gospels from the Greek: to explain the Government and
connexion of the Words; to turn English into grammatical
Latin." See "Plan of Education" incorporated as an ap-
pendix in *Statutes of Columbia College, in New York* (New
York, 1788).

maticks[6] that they are therefore inadequate to that study and generally those difficulties occasion such despair that the student has so diminutive an idea of himself as to check him greatly in the pursuit of knowledge. The study of words in the Greek language answers no better purpose than the study of them in the Dutch. 'Tis true that many valuable authors have written in the dead languages but I doubt whether there are not equally celebrated ones in the English and French languages and equally valuable . . . the study of the Moderns is of more advantage than [that] of the Ancients, especially to Modern Youth. If there are those whose genius is like that of Demosthenes, the study of the Greek may possibly be of some service to them.[7] But to real moderns the sacrifice of time will never be compensated by the benefit arising from the study of it. If four or five years of Virgil's early life had been spent in the study of languages other than his own, we should not have been favored with such excellent poetry from him so early as his twenty fourth year.
New York, December 15, 1792.

---

[6] In these essays there is frequently lack of uniformity in the spelling of certain words, such as "Mathematics," "ancient," "fountains," "critics," and so forth. With the exception of the word "waiving" (which Tompkins spelled "waving" in his essay "On Dishonesty and Extreme Indulgence") the editors have sought to reproduce all words here as spelled in the original manuscript.

[7] The author presents further arguments regarding this matter in his essay "On the Comparative Merits of Studying Classical Poetry and Prose," January 31, 1794, given here on p. 27.

On IDLENESS

. . . When we take into consideration the disadvantages which obstruct the progress of the youth in study in either [the city or the country] we find them almost to equiponderate. I am well aware that many are ready to object, that the city affords so very many allurements and enticements which attract the attention of the student and draw away his mind from study. These objections are important and ought to have their due weight; yet if any person will deny that the enticements of hunting angling and the like which the country affords are not equal inducements and equally invite the attention of the student, I must assure h[im of being deficient] in Judgment. . . .

Those inducements to pleasure and those allurements presented by a city will soon cloy and the student will turn from them and apply to study, whereas those of the country continue to attract him and his love for them encreases the more he practises them. If a student can elude the grasp of vice (and he who cannot deserves not the name of student) the matter may be decided upon with much precission; for immediately upon finding their disadvantages equal the scale of advantage preponderates in favor of the city. The benefit of libraries and the opportunity of acquiring every species of useful information give a decided preference to the city; because he who has had the advantages of these is undoubtedly capable of becoming the most useful of the two. . . .

[7]

How astonishing is it, that a student should voluntarily obstruct his own happi[ness] and that of Society! Yet how many instances do we . . . observe of men who indulge themselves in the vice of Idleness and dwell in the most slothful inactivity. Idleness is a great barrier to the acquisition of wisdom [of] wealth and of every thing which tends to the happiness of Individuals and of Society. It is the mother [of] Ignorance and Idolatry, both [of] which lead to the destruction of public and private wealth and welfare. In short the many evils which result from Idle[ness] and the train of vices which ensue in consequence of it [ought] to discourage from the practice of it. . . .
Columbia College, February 16, 1793.

On PLAYS

. . . The abolition of vice cannot be effected whilst those fountains from which immorality and vice flow are left unmolested. The most ex[peditious] way to put an end to an effect is to extinguish the cause. Is it not remarkable, then, that a prohibition of plays has not taken place long before the present time? From the play house originate as many vices and diseases as can be imagined. Pandora's box was not more full of them. What I intend is to endeavor to prove in the first place that plays are the most fruitful cause of gaming. In order to attend these plays it is necessary that a person should obtain cash sufficient to purchase a ticket for the play &c. which amounts to about three dollars per week. Most persons who attend plays the most frequently are those least inclined to labor and most prone to pleasure and of course the most indigent. Many of this description are obliged by gaming and other bad practices to procure money for the play. Besides plays give a Romantic turn to the mind which places most who attend them above plain industry. . . . *(To be continued)*

New York, March 9, 1793.

On DRUNKENNESS

. . . It is no uncharitable calculation, I suppose, that one half of the human race have in a great [measure] deserted the cause of Bacchus; have shamefully turned their [eyes from] the sparkling glass and flowing bowl; and gone in com[pany] with the beasts of the field to quench their thirst at the stream or bubbling fountain, or if at any time they [are] prevailed upon to taste the nectarious juice it is done in such a sparing and timid manner as does dishonor to the profession of drinking.

If we look back into the early ages of the world, we shall find Noah more than middling well fuddled with the produce of his new vineyard; but as we never hear of his repeating it a second time and as all his other actions are far from [revealing] him a good son of Bacchus we cannot recommend him for an example. Any man may stumble upon a good action but it is perseverance alone that merits applause. Encouraged by wine antient Lot laid the foundation of two great and populous nations Moab and the children of Ammon. And I doubt not but many honorable and useful inventions of more recent time owe their origin to the nocturnal excursions of some intriguing and adventrous Bacchanal. Alexander had natural ferocity enough to deal death and destruction through the world among those he called his enemies, but to wine alone he was indebted for that generous and noble ardour which enabled him to stab and murder his most faithful and affectionate friends. To wine alone he surrendered his pretended immortality which was nothing more than a particular kind of Drunkenness. But we need not search the pages of antiquity for examples to recommend this water of life. The many advantages arising from a full stomach and a racking head will be evident to any who will but make the experiment. Nay less than experience—observation alone will [serve] our turn. . . . How often do we see him [the drunkard] by some interior [cause] extending his jaws and bursting into thundering laughter without any of those exterior causes which generally provoke the sober soul to [laugh]. But this is not all;

Drunkenness will also effectually purge away the fool-
ish sympathy which a person would otherwise feel for
human nature in distress, so that if a man find it necessary for the good order of his house that his wife should
be kicked out of doors [or] for the support of his
funds that his neighbours throat should be cut and his
money transferred into his own chest, a plentiful
draught of good West India will enable him to perform either the one or the other with as much Bravery
and unrelenting fury as if he had lived among the
infernals. And after all how little need he regard law,
justice [or] the worst consequences that can possibly
ensue; a plentiful potion of the same liquor which
helped him to commit the action will embolden him
undauntedly [to] encounter the punishment to which
it may expose him. And if it should cost him his life
death is an evil we all must encounter etc.

For your encouragement ye heroes of the bottle—
attend to the issue of this fortunate man. He shall be
endowed as it were with the spirit of prophecy and be
able to predict the very day and manner of his death.
At his last hour he shall be punctually waited upon by
the officers of the state and a numerous train of lower
order. While others are walking on foot he shall be
born[e] in a Vehicle with a particular badge of honor
about his neck and lastly he shall swing away his life
in airy circles without a groan or a sigh raised aloft
above the gaping and admiring not to say envying
world.

New York, March 22, 1793.

On ORATORY

ORATORY is one of the greatest and most useful acquisitions that a man is capable of. Every endeavor to improve young gentlemen in it, is, in the highest degree commendable. Nothing can be more incumbent on and more beneficial to a person in a country like ours than an incessant study and exercise of Eloquence. Hence in almost all the seminaries of learning where the principal branches of knowlege are intended to be taught, Speaking constitutes a considerable part of the students duty.

The intent of speaking in these institutions I suppose principally is to habituate young gentlemen to proper pronunciation and emphasis in the delivery of an oration—to regulate their gestures and to teach them to express the various passions in a natural and proper manner. My design at present was to enquire whether a student could accomplish these ends as compleatly by speaking his own composition, which he may have written whilst in some of the lower or middle classes. Proper pronunciation he may be taught altho' he speak his own performance; but I doubt at the same time whether his improvement will be in the pronunciation of the most elegant and proper words, unless a student in college may be supposed to use words equally well chosen and proper as a good orator or judicious author, which I am persuaded is very seldom the case.

It will be found that in examining the performance of a student ambiguous sentences will frequently occur. Young men are prone to think confusedly and inaccurately and not plainly to perceive the object they intend to describe and consequently to express themselves with intricacy and obscurity. Here the person before whom he speaks must be at a loss where to place the emphasis for the speakers benefit. The method of frequently composing cannot be too much inculcated, but I am inclined to believe that when the object of improvement in speaking is in view, the most salutary consequences will be found to result from the choice of the best executed performances [of some able orator].

New York, April 6, 1793.

On SLAVERY: I

THE PRESENT CENTURY has exhibited to the world some characters, actions, and events that are not equalled in history. Perhaps the mind of man never felt such a thirst for knowlege as for a few years past; and as knowlege hath expanded their minds, they began to consider the nature and foundation of government, and this consideration led them to see their slavery and gave them a taste for Liberty. Struggles have ensued which gave field for the display of those actions and events which will be recorded whilst Freedom endures.

Happy for America that she has been successful in her struggle for Liberty, but unhappy that she has not fully completed her design altho' it was in her power to have done it. It would seem that the inhabitants of this Country have not that innate love for Liberty which many of them profess; otherwise we should not behold our fellow creatures in Slavery when it is in our power to relieve them. Liberty naturally fits and qualifies us for improvement in knowlege and knowlege allures us to, and gives us a relish for "Th' ineffable delights of sweet humanity." Among those who are free and enlightened, if one man promote the happiness of another, his own delight is increased in the same ratio; and no man can enjoy real felicity whilst he beholds others miserable.

These observations I thought proper to make before I entered on the subject I designed to write upon. In my next composition I shall endeavor to enquire what can be offered by free citizens to excuse them for retaining slaves and also to show the impropriety and inhumanity of Slavery.

New York, June 22, 1793.

On SLAVERY : II

IT WOULD BE an unpopular attempt to endeavor to prove, that colour is the [chief] objection against the Africans, to prevent them from associating and intermarrying with European and American inhabitants. To throw a veil over their conducts the purchasers of human creatures profess to believe that the Slaves have not natural powers and endowments equal to those who lord it over them and hence no doubt originates much of the brutal treatment they receive. But Nature has made little or no distinction in the *original* make of men's minds or their natural endowments. The difference is principally and I may say totally to be ascribed to culture and a *proper application* of the powers of their minds. Of this, the difference of civilization of different nations is a striking proof; and that the same nation has been at one time celebrated for learning and knowledge and at another enveloped in Ignorance. I cannot doubt but that local prejudices assist in confirming many in this belief. But the distinction which subsists relative to ability might be rationally accounted for on the score of their seclusion from intercourse with civilized persons, their abject slavery, and their cruel usage; for despondency and grossest Ignorance necessarily ensue.

To account for the Colour of the unhappy creatures is what I shall n[ot] attempt at present *to perform*. Reason instructs us that they are not [to] be blamed on that account. Custom has caused us to look upon them with disdain, but we ought to consider that the "Leopard cannot change his spots." Where intercourse with them is reputable we find, as in the West Indies, that very honourable and happy connections are found with them.

So far have some persons strained the point that they have even ventured to pronounce them the descendants of Cain and have therefore forfeited their freedom. Fiction will have great influence on men and especially credit is given to what flatters our wishes and promotes our interest. But I flatter myself this bare supposition is derived from a Source which justifies me in making no defence.

It requires the pen of Sterne[8] to paint the horrors of Slavery and shew the miseries of slaves. But it would require a more than mortal effort, to exculpate the descendants of Europe from the just imputation of Savage Barbarity.—

(To be continued)

New York, June 28, 1793.

---

[8] Laurence Sterne (1713-68), in his "The Captive, Paris," sets down his thoughts on slavery as he watches a starling captive in a cage.—*The Works of Sterne*, Philadelphia, 1870, II (Sentimental Journey through France and Italy), 70-71.

On THE DEVELOPMENT OF THE ARTS AND SCIENCES IN AMERICA

IT CANNOT BUT delight every lover of his Country to view the rapid advances which it is making towards the perfection of the arts and Sciences. Never did a country excite greater expectation of future greatness than America. Free from the ravages of war she supports an extensive trade abroad; and her inland trade is preferable to all Countries in the world because of the extent of back Country and the numerous navigable lakes and Rivers, that flow through all parts of the Continent. The enjoyment of a temperate and healthful climate encourages industry and promotes the Agricultural Interest. The Agricultural Interest is at present that on which the principal dependance of this Country lies; But the many improvements in Mechanism give flattering prospects that the Course of a century will bring it to the highest state of perfection it has ever known.

Exclusive of these national [*sic*] advantages the improvements in Civilization, the Cultivation of the mind and the general diffusion of useful knowlege give the most sanguine hopes of future grandeur. These can outlive the ravages of War. An extensive diffusion of knowlege implants a desire to excell and this desire prompts to virtuous and praiseworthy conduct. Knowledge diffused among all ranks checks the oppression of aspiring Governments.

In War we have given demonstrations of our firmness and valour and we have equally obtained admiration by the wisdom of our Legislators, our philosophers and poets and the cultivation of the arts of peace.

To enjoy a free government and enlightened fellow-citizens is one advance towards happiness and these invaluable blessings we prize according to the rich price with which they were purchased.

> Oh! Liberty thou Goddess heavenly bright
> Profuse of bliss, and pregnant with delight
> Eternal pleasures in thy presence reign
> And smiling Plenty leads thy wanton train
> Thou mak'st the gloomy face of Nature gay
> Giv'st beauty to the sun, and pleasure to the day.[9]

New York, July 27, 1793.

---

[9] Joseph Addison (1672-1719), in "A Letter from Italy. To the Right Hon. Charles Lord Halifax, in the Year 1701." Two lines which Tompkins omitted and which immediately follow "And smiling Plenty leads thy wanton train" are these:
  "Eas'd of her load Subjection grows more light,
  And Poverty looks cheerful in thy sight."
Works of the English Poets from Chaucer to Cowper, London, 1810, IX, 530-31.

New York. July 27.

It cannot but delight every lover of his
Country to view the rapid advances which it is
making towards the perfection of the arts and
Sciences. Never did a country afford excite greater
expectations of future greatness than America. —
Free from the ravages of War she supports an exten
sive trade abroad, and her inland trade is preferable to all Countries in the world because of
the extent of back Country & the numerous
navigable lakes and Rivers, that flow through
all parts of the Continent. The enjoyment of
a temperate and healthful climate encourages
industry & promotes the Agricultural Interest.
The Agricultural Interest is at present that
on which the principal dependance of this
Country lies; But the many improve-

PAGE FROM THE ORIGINAL MANUSCRIPT OF THE ESSAY
ON THE DEVELOPMENT OF THE ARTS AND SCIENCES
IN AMERICA (REDUCED)

On ACQUIRING A KNOWLEDGE OF LANGUAGE and THE RULES OF GOOD WRITING

. . . The superficial [attention] which we in general bestow on acquiring the knowlege of language and of the rules of good writing plainly demonstrates that we either do not consult or criminally neglect our truest interest. There are many inducements to in[vite] us to this study whilst we are young—it is not difficult or abstruse, but delightful. However I am not of opinion, that we ought to be put to the task of composing, until we have obtained an acquaintance with Blair's[10] lectures and some knowledge of Mathematicks, Logic and the languages. The reasons which evince this previous knowlege to be necessary are obvious. Without it any person will undoubtedly think incorrectly and of course express himself ambiguously. This incorrect manner of thinking and bad stile will grow into a habit, from which, (however he may afterwards study to avoid it) he cannot easily refrain.

At an immature age we are apt to prefer what is

---

[10] Hugh Blair (1718-1800), Scotch divine, and professor of rhetoric at the University of Edinburgh. His *Lectures on Rhetoric and Belles-Lettres* was first published in 1783, when he resigned his professorship. A tenth edition appeared in 1806. For widely differing estimates of Blair and the *Lectures* see C. W. Moulton ed., *Library of Literary Criticism of English and American Authors*, New York, 1935, IV, 403-7.

shewy and glaring to that which is simple, and are desirous to imitate it. Hence we chuse a subject of importance, of which we have few solid ideas and are prone to supply the deficiency by pomposity of expression which leads us into the worst stile in the world—the Frigid stile.

Figurative language possesses something that captivates us, and the desire of acquiring a figurative stile is laudable, but unless we are instructed by reading in our choice and [arrangement] of figures we shall make but a ridiculous appearance. . . .

Let us in the meantime study assiduously Mathematicks and [engage in] the reading of useful books to supply and correctly arrange materials, and Belle lettres and the languages to adorn them and express ourselves with elegance and propriety; and then we shall be possessed of the means of chosing and acquiring a good habit. I know not what prompts us to it, but as an excuse for inattention, I have hugged myself in an idea, that when occasion offered I could write well, but I am at length undeceived in this for when I have attempted it, "I tugg'd and sweat and toil'd in vain." Our pride induces us to leave the lower sorts of stile and our idleness renders us unfit for the higher, hence "Dum vitat humum, nubes et inania captat" when we abandon the humble stile we soar in air. These being a few of the many disadvantages arising from the ignorance of the Bellettres does it not behoove us speedily to obtain a knowledge of them and tho' now we may esteem some things they teach as trifling and puerile a few years will convince us that they are infinitely interesting. Let us therefore instead of despising this study, pay strict attention to Blairs lectures and books in the languages on this subject. Let us "Read them by day, and study them by night." Consider what ideas we shall have hereafter concerning our present opportunities—what an appearance we shall make in the world and of what trifling benefit we shall be to mankind or even to ourselves. At a future period how shall we blame and even despise ourselves for the total neglect of privileges which we should all think inestimable! But alas! . . .

August 23, 1793.

On CAPITAL PUNISHMENT

I SHALL FIRST [attempt] to shew the impolicy of the punishment of death and that it does not accomplish what is designed thereby; and mention some punishments which may be substituted in its stead, less cruel but in the end tending more to prevent the commission of crimes; and to make satisfaction for the injury done; for I presume punishments are inflicted with one of these intentions, either to compensate for the injury or to deter others from the commission of crimes. That where the more rigid punishments are dispensed with, crimes will be less frequent is a truth sanctioned by the experience of some of the most civilized countries, and that the fewer instances there are of executions the greater effect they will have when they do take place and vice versa. Hence they are inadequate to deter from crimes. If a man deprives me of property etc. what satisfaction can I receive from his death, unless I am transported with cruel revenge. By servitude he might make me reparation at least in part; he might contribute also to the support of his [family]. . . .[11]

(To be continued)

New York, November 15, 1793.

On THE DIFFICULTY OF WRITING COMPOSITION

. . . Without ruminating well upon a subject we expect to write with merit. . . . When we sit down to write we perceive a deficiency [and] are apt to attribute it to the choice of an unsuitable subject. If we feel embarassed and unable to proceed [on] one

---

[11] On numerous occasions during his public career Tompkins vigorously protested against capital punishment. Some of his most eloquent utterances while governor were in support of more humane penalties.

subject we reject that and engage upon another and [it] not unfrequently happens that a train of subjects follows each other on the paper [e.g.:] "Nothing is more detestable than drunkeness"—Here we pause to consider what else to say and at length draw a black line under those words and begin anew. "Among the many vices to which mankind are subject nothing has a more extensively bad influence than intemperance." Inability to proceed gracefully on that subject induces to begin with a new line. "When we consider the disadvantages arising from Intemperance"—when perhaps the clock strikes nine. Want of time obliges us then to take refuge in some old thread bare subject as Capital punishment, etc.; A pitiful refuge! but it may prevent the incurring of fines. On these subjects enough has been written by others to furnish us with materials for one side down and two or three lines at the top of the second page. This being accomplished, all we have to do is to close as well as we are able by a "(to be continued)."

New York, Nov. 23rd, 1793.

On NOVELS

The first lines are in part illegible; but their substance is that Tompkins had at an early age imbibed the idea that novels are

. . . solely for the amusement of puerile minds. Nor did I imbibe this idea from my own voluntary choice but by reason of an injunction laid upon me by one of my . . . teachers, that I should "carefully avoid reading novels." This *false* notion of his, as I now think it, must certainly have arisen from preacquired prejudices; and so he would not leave me to taste for myself, but would taste for me. As children by their catechisms are taught to admit principles as true without being convinced of the truth of them as they ought to be by their own reason; they have faculties given them as well as others to reason with and in time may use them as well, and in consequence of conviction from reasoning only ought they to establish principles like these; but on the contrary many of them may be said not to profess their own religion but that of their minister, and I believe it is frequently the case, that they retain prejudicions in favor of certain principles for life, which, had they been weighed by their own unbiassed reasoning, they would have deemed erroneous. By prejudices, derived from causes similar to these, I am confident many have deprived themselves of the pleasure and benefit of reading some of the productions of the most soaring geniuses that ever the world produced. The idea of a good novel carries with it the idea of genius; because the admirable faculty of invention is among the Chief req[uisites of the novelist]. . . . Among some [of the] novels at present extant, there be but few good ones, [which] is an evidence that they are to be ranked among the most difficult species of writing.

It is not unfrequently observed by the enemies of novels, that they are mere Fiction and representations of things that never have and perhaps never will exist; and what then? Fiction when applied to novels is the same thing as invention and it is this that gives novels such a superiority over other writings. Besides it appears to me, that those who use this objection Mistake the true design and intent of novels; they are representations of men and things, qualified to excite to the love of virtue and detestation of vice; and Fiction gives room for painting them in deeper colours, than when we are confined to real characters. In short as in poetry, painting and statuary individual Nature may be excelled, so also in novels; by combining the excellences of many characters in one, we may excite our love for Virtue more than by confining ourselves to the real excellencies of any one character only. But yet it is Fiction and this word, especially among superstitious people, seems to carry a bad idea with it; and on this account we must forbear reading them. . . .

It is further remarked, that novels have a bad tendency, by possessing a power of alluring the reader and cause him to devote his whole attention to them. Mathematicks it is observed have the same tendency to those who have a relish for the pleasure arising from that study, yet in my humble opinion, this is not a sufficient demonstration to shew, that Mathematicks ought to be avoided. In fact this very power to attract the reader is what we require in all writings, but if we are guilty of a vicious extreme we ought to blame our own weakness and not the good qualities of the book.

New York, January 11 [*perhaps 1794*].

On PREJUDICE

. . . In short if we look into the world, we shall find few men utterly free from prejudice of one kind or another. Local attachments, habit and the like frequently beget and nourish prejudice. I know many who are of this and the other profession in Religion and [profess] a substantial reason for it too, to witt, that their fathers before them were of that same profession. Yet subject as we all are, to be duped by Prejudice, the least appearance of it in others excites our disgust. When we find the historian swayed by prejudice in the relation of facts all our pleasure of reading him is diminished. . . .

New York, January 18, 1794.

On THE COMPARATIVE MERITS OF STUDYING CLASSICAL POETRY AND PROSE

HE WHO ATTEMPTS to censure or shew the expediency of Rules which general practice has established, is not likely to make many converts or acquire many friends; especially if those regulations are sanctioned and adopted by the learned. On which account I do not flatter myself with an idea of much success, in endeavoring to convince that the practice of our most eminent teachers of the Classics, in assigning Poetic rather than prose authors for the study of Youth, is not the most conducive to benefit, or a speedy acquisition of those languages. Let the object of the student be, either to acquire a knowledge of the language or to obtain ideas from the ancient authors, prose writings I am persuaded will best conduce to the accomplishment of their wishes.

The less time we consume in acquiring those languages the better. For which reason that species of writing which leads us by the shortest path to the obtaining them ought certainly to be preferred. Unless we attempt to acquire a thorough knowledge of all the words in the language, an acquaintance with those words which were most commonly used by the ancients themselves, will be found to be the best, and such I imagine are those most generally used by their prose writers. It is also very probable that the greater part of our words formed from those languages, are derived from such words of most common use amongst them. The principal attainment in studying their poetic writings, is, a knowlege of the exquisite harmony of numbers, of which their language was so highly susceptible, and an exalted idea of the great Genius of the authors; neither of them lending much to the improvement of the understanding, nor should we be able on account of the properties of our language, in any great degree to imitate their harmony. It is most beneficial to gain such ideas as will best prepare us for performing the duties of Life, and of becoming useful to society and such we ought to be solicitous to acquire. By every one who wishes to attain eminence in Oratory, the writings of the ancients, are most worthy to be consulted. In their prose writings, instructions for improvement in Eloquence are principally found. In construing a prose author, we pay more attention to the sense or to his ideas than in reading poetry, and a practice of reading prose authors when young, will

32

Newyork January 31st...

He who attempts to censure or shew the
[...] of Rules which general practice has established is not likely to make many converts or acquire
many friends, especially if those regulations are
sanctioned and adopted by the learned. On
which account I do not flatter myself with an
idea of much success, in endeavouring to convince
that the practice of our most eminent teachers of the
Classics, in assigning Poetic rather than prose
authors for the study of Youth, is not the most
conducive to benefit, or a speedy acquisition of those
languages. Let the object of the student be, either
to acquire a knowledge of the language or to obtain
ideas from the ancient authors, prose writings I am
persuaded will best conduce to the accomplishment of their wishes.

The less time we consume in acquiring those languages the better. For which reason that species
of writing which leads us by the shortest path
to the attaining them ought certainly to be pre-

PAGE FROM THE ORIGINAL MANUSCRIPT OF THE ESSAY
ON THE COMPARATIVE MERITS OF STUDYING
CLASSICAL POETRY AND PROSE (REDUCED)

promote a facility of understanding their writings with respect to the sense when we are older. In Poetry it is quite otherwise. Whilst our whole attention is confined to the numerous licenses of the poets, to additions and abbreviations [e.g.:] Boeotice, Attice, Ionice, Poetice etc., as a late author observes "the sense evaporates."[12]

(To be continued)

New York, January 31, 1794.

On DISHONESTY *and*
EXTREME INDULGENCE

THERE ARE NO vices more common or more mischievous in their nature than dishonesty and extreme Indulgence of pleasure. Some have imagined that Honesty is not the best policy, as far as it regards this life and that a profuse gratification of sense affords more happiness than a moderate, temperate indulgence of pleasure. Were it possible for a man really to disbelieve Futurity, which many eminent men actually deny, and, were we to suppose mans total existence confined to this life, I doubt whether dishon-

---

[12] In the Boeotian, Attic, and Ionic manners, or dialects. The word "Poetice" as here used is probably equivalent to "Homeric."

esty or intemperate gratification would be found beneficial to the individual himself. In Society, every member is bound by the most sacred ties to preserve Harmony and the Tranquility of all the community. This consideration sufficiently evinces the perniciousness of Dishonesty. Besides whatever success Knavery may find for once, it will find it difficult to succeed a second time, for one imposition places all on their guard, and affixes a mark of infamy, which causes the person to be universally shunned. Prodigality generally accompanies dishonesty; and soon consumes what an act of Knavery has acquired. He is therefore reduced to the necessity of having recourse a second time to dishonesty. But as I said before, he will find all prepared for his attack—And even tho' he should find it necessary to deal for once with probity, he will find none to negotiate with him. For when the wind blows from one quarter we commonly expect it to continue there for some time. It may be said that, in order to be expert in dishonesty, the world must be imposed on by an appearance of probity. But the world bad as it may be, will soon detect the hypocrite, and stigmatize him as his infamy deserves. The effect of these disappointments, is that he either falls into poverty and wretchedness; or, has recourse to acts of violence and meets the punishment the laws of the country require.

Experience will shew, that those who plunge into an indiscriminate and unlimited gratification of sensual appetites are perfectly intoxicated. Those who imagine that such persons enjoy more Felicity than the moderate and temperate are sadly plunged in error. For wa[i]ving the consideration of Futurity, they forgot that by an immoderate use, the organs of enjoyment become as it were blunted, and incapable of giving Felicity. Besides, sensual indulgence debilitates the body, enervates the faculties of the soul and disqualifies [a man] to perform those duties which are essential to his own happiness, and which are due to society in general. He deprives his posterity of the support they naturally expect, and squanders upon those least deserving of it. Is it possible for a man in such circumstances to be exempt from the most piercing reflection? In short without moderation and temperance in pleasure nature has made us *rational* in vain, and we rise but little above the brute creation.

New York, February 21 [*1794*].

On GOVERNMENT: I

The opening sentences, partly illegible, assert that there are two sides to every question, including that of monarchy as a desirable or undesirable form of government. From that point the author proceeds as follows:

[31]

. . . The material argument to support monarchy seems to be its antiquity; and the reasons which induced men at that period to adopt it are urged in its defence now. That monarchy was the most ancient form of government all historians agree and the [reason] for this is obvious. Mankind found themselves under the necessity [of creating or maintaining] order of some kind in Society, and as it is to be presumed [were] ignorant and unacquainted with government except in families, that government which bore the nearest resemblance to the authority which fathers ex[erted] over their children, was undoubtedly the first assented to. Their ignorance and prejudice prevented them from changing their government when experience had given them some notions of republics. But mankind at that period it is to be presumed had made but inconsiderable advance in civilization and were as yet ignorant and savage; on which account their having adopted Monarchy as a government cannot tend to recommend it, since that they instituted this form may be imputed totally to their ignorance and uncivilized state; because as mankind increased in civilization and knowlege, Monarchy was thrown off and a republican form of government established in its stead. This we cannot doubt if we credit history which informs us that Athens and Rome were monarchies at first.

The design of Government is to insure the tranquility of the members of the Community. Kingly governments, it must be acknowledged are most inclined to war. Hence the subjects of that government are kept poor. That which they have a right to, in order to subsistence and happiness, is extorted from them to support a war which has no object but to gratify the ambition and promote the fame of their Monarch. The former and present monarchs in Europe have pursued the same method of governing and scarce a prince who lives to a considerable age dies without having declared three or four wars during his reign.

Where one person possesses the prerogatives of Royalty, those who are subordinate will endeavour to imitate him and from the reverence they have acquired for him, esteem all his actions patterns for them. Hence a dissolute and vicious King will make a corrupt and debauched nation. And where crowns are hereditary it [is likely] that such will frequently possess them. . . . [The] propriety of a son's succeeding his father, we are informed is [to prevail] because it is to be presumed that he has received the advantages of his father's wise instructions and imbibed his noble sentiments and therefore is best qualified for the office. Let us suppose Cicero to have been a king in an hereditary government, under whose wise instructions his son Marcus lived. We are therefore to conclude according to their method of drawing inferences, that Marcus would be the most proper person to succeed his father when history universally declares that Marcus was a mere blockhead.

(To be continued)

[*March 17, 1794?*].

On GOVERNMENT: II

Tompkins is stressing the desirability of placing in public office only those persons who possess "wisdom and virtue."

. . . This rule for evident reasons seldom is complied with in a Monarchy. A wicked prince *will* not choose a wise and virtuous officer, lest he should detect and expose his infamy, and a weak prince is not qualified to distinguish wisdom from folly or vice from Virtue.

It is by no means a recommendation to a monarchial form of Government, that luxury is inseperable from it. This possesses greater weight, when we reflect that Luxury, which has a most unhappy influence on Society, is inconsistent with and tends to overthrow a republican Government. It is universally true that Luxury diminishes human happiness: Hence on the one hand the virtuous part of mankind are naturally inclined to detest a form of government, one of whose supports is founded on so deplorable a basis and to give their approbation to that form, with which Luxury is incompatible.

In disputation, it is not uncommon to misconstrue and pervert the phrases of our opponents. This has not failed to happen on this subject.[13] But it may be remarked that whenever one who defends a cause, has recourse to so mean a subterfuge, we must suspect that he either does not possess abilities adequate to the defence of his cause by fair and candid reasoning, or, what is more probable, that his side of the question is so bad and barren of good argument that he is obliged to have recourse to cavilling. Equality has been taken and I presume designedly to reduce all to a promiscuous level. [In this] sense I imagine we may understand, that all [those for] whose benefit governments are instituted and made should have an equal right to a share in forming [them], an equal right to their protection to the benefits resulting from them. In fact we may take the definition of it by a famous author as a good one, "That equality does not consist in managing so that every body should command but in obeying and commanding our Equals." Nothing is more inconsistent with the

---

[13] During the period within which these essays fall, this subject was a very live one in American politics. Jefferson and his followers were fearful that the Federalist leaders, particularly Alexander Hamilton and John Adams, were seeking to undermine republican government in the United States and to establish a monarchical form similar to that in England.

true spirit of Equality, than that *extreme equality,* which many attempt to intermingle and confound with true Equality.

I shall not endeavour to prove that Monarchy is a bad form of government, provided the people can have a good King because I imagine, that in my last I shewed, that this is extremely improbable where Kings are elected and in hereditary governments utterly impossible; for universal experience evinces, that a person educated and brought up at Court seldom possesses wisdom and is generally destitute of religion and virtue.

I shall conclude with some thoughts of the celebrated Montesquieu[14] on Monarchy. "Let us compare (says he) what the historians of all ages have declared concerning the courts of Monarchs; let us recollect the conversations and sentiments of peoples of all countries with respect to the wretched character of Courtiers and we shall find that they are not mere airy speculations, but things confirmed by a sad and melancholy experience."

(To be continued)

New York, April 5, 1794.

---

[14] Charles Louis de Secondat, Baron de la Brède et de Montesquieu (1689-1755), author of *L'Esprit des lois,* which dealt with law in general, forms of government, manners and customs, feudal law, religion, and so forth. From this highly significant work American statesmen who engaged in setting up the new government during and following the American Revolution derived suggestions which supplemented colonial experience. One of the most notable contri-

In what may have been a rough draught of the above essay Tompkins has stated somewhat more fully his views regarding equality as follows:

. . . Equality has been taken and I imagine designedly too in a sense very foreign from what the adherents of republican governments or the most strict democrats would define it, namely to reduce all to a level. True it is that all men are *naturally* equal . . . but this equality being incompatible society is in a manner lost and men become equal in the political sense, namely that all citizens for whose benefit laws are enacted have an equal right to a share in forming them and an equal right to their protection and of benefits arising from them. We may take the celebrated Montesquieu's definition of Equality as a good one. As distant as is heaven from Earth (says he) so is [the] true spirit of equality from that of extreme equality. . . .

On JUVENILE SOCIETIES

The organizations herein described had for their chief object the improvement of the members' work in com-

---

butions which Montesquieu seems to have made to American governmental theory and practice was with respect to the separation of powers.

position. "That, at least," wrote Tompkins, "is what most of them have in view at the time of their institution." After the opening sentences, now in part illegible, the author proceeds:

. . . Perhaps my disgust for these associations may acquire me the name of a morose misanthropist. But I would rather combat with these reproaches than encourage delusion; for experience and reason convince me that to the attainment of the above end, these institutions are inadequate. Those of them which have the improvement of stile and eloquence in view as an object, are to be commended in this, that they are in pursuit of a laudable design, but to be commiserated in that they mistake the *means* of accomplishing it.

No society can accomplish the design of its institution, or be of long duration, whose laws do not promote union and intimate connection between the members, and establish the promotion of the association as the interest and duty of each member. But the individuals composing it should be united in the pursuit of the same object and be restrained to a decent deportment. To these ends the constitution and laws should directly tend. In the formation of such a constitution and such laws much experience, penetration and judgment are required. Now I submit it to the judicious to decide, whether persons of the age of fifteen or sixteen years, can construct for themselves these necessary preservatives of their existence and whether they can execute them with firm and unshaken equity?

Experience daily confirms that no person is calculated to teach a branch, in which he is not thoroughly instructed himself. Now, in order to improve a compo[sition] an able and judicious instructor should be assigned, who will supply the place of a friend and critick—a critic to trace out . . . the blemishes both in sentiment and stile, [and offer guidance] in the choice of subjects. . . . The flights of imagination may be indulged and encouraged, but without the assistance of true criticism youth will pursue them with too much ardor without regard to their suitableness perhaps either to time or place.

Hence, unless the members of a youthful association, can be presumed to have extensive and true knowledge of Belles-lettres and criticisms, they will prove *carping* and not judicious criticks. Whether this authority to examine and correct composition be vested in the president, a select committee, or the society at large, we may promise ourselves but little utility from their profound animadversions. Not long since, I had the honor to belong to an association to whose perusal I submitted a composition, that had been previously corrected by the president of a respectable seminary and recopied. It was laughable to behold, the president of this Honourable body, leaving the most part unmolested and directing his merciless talons at those very corrections,

which the first mentioned president had previously
made, recorrecting and re-amending them, and
learnedly and elaborately pointing out to me his
manifest mistakes and errors! And have I lived to behold the era, when the abilities of a respectable professor of the Belles-lettres, should be araigned at
the tribunal of the president of an obscure association and yet fail to despise such ridiculous self importance? . . . [Money obtained by the society
from fines, etc. might well] be appropriated to em-
ploy a man of eminence in Literature; who should
preside in our debates, correct [our] compositions,
and have cognizance of our conduct. He should be
authorized to interrupt a member speaking, to explain to him, wherein he advanced things foreign to
his present subject—shew him how he might have
adjusted his arguments in an order, calculated to
make the strongest impression and that afterwards
he should recapitulate the whole subject in as able
and masterly a manner as he could, to afford his
pupils examples to illustrate his remarks. That he
should solemnly regard the equitable distribution of
praise and censure to those whose performances were
deserving of either, thus establishing a kind of criterion for merit, to which they could resort. This respectability of the teacher would insure confidence
in his remarks and excite a laudable emulation in
each to merit his encomiums. Besides his perpetuity
of office would prevent those tumults and convul-

sions in societies, which happen at elections etc., when ambitious and disappointed members will be assidious to sew divisions and cause a separation. Which *reason* accounts for the many divisions and subdivisions of societies and for the great number at present in this city, more noted for their number and pompous manner than for their respectability. . . .[15]

New York, July 10, 1794.

On RURAL LIFE IN RELATION
TO POETRY

. . . If solitude and retirement are [agreeable] to the cultivation of poetic genius, the country is the favorite residence of the muses or [if] the objects of nature afford more copious topics for the poets pen than those [of the city] we cannot wonder that rural scenes should so captivate the poets. Serenity and Contentment, a mind free from turbulent passions and a good heart are necessary qualifications for a good poet. The contemplation of the objects of Nature, displayed in rural scenes, produce cheerfulness and diffuse calmness and

---

[15] Among the more prominent social and political (but non-literary) societies in New York City at this time were the Democratic Society and the Tammany Society.

serenity over the mind. It is universally believed that the peasant possesses more Virtue and innocence than almost any other description of men whatever. This arises from the place he resides in and the peculiar influence his employment has upon his body and mind. Health flows from exercise and temperance and excludes those disquietudes which attend the intemperate and infirm; and being secluded from the riotous crowd he less frequently has his viler passions roused. Besides the works of nature strike the rustic more sensibly than the citizen and penetrate him with lively sentiments of gratitude to his creator. This is a natural inducement to check the rise of passion and gradually meliorates and refines the heart of man.

But I am inclined to think that the partiality of the poets for rural scenes arises from that extent which they give the imagination and Fancy to rove in; and that they afford perpetual instances of the sublime and beautiful. A morning walk in the Country will [afford] ample materials for poetic description . . . objects that excite an admiration and delight. [From] the summit of a hill, we have a prospect of the [extensive and variegated] landscapes, wide forests and winding vales and the distant mountains whose blue tops seem to lose themselves in the clouds, or [we] find ourselves on the brink of a high nod[ding] precipice. If we descend into the vally we pass thro' bowers and arches of trees thickly interwoven by nature's hand and affording a pleasing melancholy gloom and by rivulets and fountains from whence the streams "dissolve harmoniously away." [We] hear roarings of torrents and the harmonious music of the feathered tribes and the verdure and exquisite colours and odours of plants and flowers at once gratify the eye and charm the ear. Thus order beauty and sublimity alternately present themselves to our view.[16]

Thompson is the most remarkable instance of a poet in whom the contemplation of rural scenes has refined the imagination and passions and had a happier influence on the heart. No person but one of his delicate and refined imagination could have described the scenes he did with so little offence to modesty and delicacy; and none but a good man could have so applied the objects of nature to excite our praise to the great author of them. I shall conclude with the words of this author on the variety and beauty of the seasons

> Mysterious round! What skill, what force divine
> Deep felt in these appear! A simple train,
> Yet so delightful mix'd, with such kind art
> Such beauty and beneficence combined
> Shade unperceived so softening into shade
> And all so forming an harmonious whole
> That, as they still succeed, they ravish still.

New York, August 9, 1794.

---

[16] On the cover of the essay appear a number of rather crudely drawn sketches of birds and a squirrel.

On KNOWLEDGE

Wherein Tompkins discusses the Whisky Insurrection.
A few lines of this essay are partially illegible. It is
clear, however, that in them Tompkins has made some
generalizations regarding the "fatal effects" of ignor-
ance; he continues:

. . . Hence it has been established as a maxim that in
all republicks in order to insure compliance with the
requisitions of Government knowledge ought to be
generally disseminated. If a man possesses Liberty and
has not discretion to make proper use of it, he is more
unfortunate than he who is buried in ignorance and
slavery and suffers those who possess knowlege to direct
for him.

Those inhabitants of Pennsylvania who adhere so
obstinately to their determination of opposing the Exe-
cution and preventing the operation of Law[17] are by no
means well informed citizens. Perhaps on account of
their ignorance and superstition a great part of their

---

[17] More specifically, Hamilton's Excise Act of 1791, impos-
ing a tax on distilled spirits. The measure was so unpopular
in Western Pennsylvania, where the manufacture of whisky
simplified the disposal of surplus grain and provided a con-
venient medium of exchange, that obstruction to enforce-
ment there in 1794 resulted in President Washington's use of
coercion to secure obedience to the act. That New England
more readily accepted the excise was largely due to the fact
that hard cider, a favorite drink among New England farmers,
remained untaxed.

opposition arises from the name, because an *Excise* was one of those Grievances complained of by the American Colonies at the commencement of the late war. For the same reason a stamp act among such would be a most unpopular thing, tho' that, as well as the excise law are doubtless very proper and would be attended with salutary consequences. For the ignorance and obstinacy of those citizens we may probably blame the Government who promoted the population of that part of Pennsylvania. It is natural to suppose that persons who remove to a wild [region inhabited by savages might revert to some] degree of Barbarism. To prevent this it should always be provided, that new settlements should have the means of obtaining Education and of imbibing the true principles of Religion and morality established amongst them. To the want of this foresight in the government of Pennsylvania we may probably impute the present disturbance there. The Eastern States I am informed acted very judiciously in this particular; they did not dispose of their lands except those who applied for a Township would become obligated to introduce such a number of good settlers into it, that they should support a clergyman build a house for public worship and maintain a Town School. Thus these uncultivated parts of their State instead of being the haunt of the savage and ignorant, soon became respectable and furnished persons among the best and wisest of their citizens.

People who were well informed and deliberate

would not meditate an insurrection except in the most extreme cases and not even then without having first tried all legal measures to obtain a removal of their Grievances. But above all they would first thoroughly consider whether the thing complained of was actually such an aggravating [burden as to justify revolt.] I will endeavour to investigate [this subject further] in my next composition.

September 13, 1794.

On SUITABLE COURSES OF STUDY: I

. . . To make a just estimate of our [talents] and rightly to determine for what science our genius [is] fitted and in which we are most likely to excel is one [of] the most difficult and at the same time one of the constant concerns of life. In order to extend the ability and usefulness of institutions for teaching them this observation ought to attract the regard of those who have the direction and management of them. Students seldom possess the same inclinations for any particular science or the same natural Genius. And yet the same course of study and reading is generally assigned to all,[18] and perhaps has been the means of

[18] While Tompkins was a student at Columbia College the

concealing from the world many who possessed genius nothing inferior to many who have astonished Mankind with their productions. It is said, that the circumstance which discovered the bent of Sir Isaac Newton's mind and enabled him to apply to the study in which he was afterwards so eminent was merely casual. Two of the first geniuses of the last and perhaps of any age were remarkable for the difference of their improvements in Knowledge. Pope arrived at a very early period in life, to his height of intellectual splendour; whilst on the contrary the talents of Swift were concealed for many years; so much so that whilst at the University he was generally reputed a dunce; yet his productions have abundantly convinced the world that he was equal if not superior in genius to [Pope. . . . The subjects assigned] to the one at that period were suitable to him and of course he pursued them with pleasure and delight; whilst on the other hand those allotted to the other did not comport with his talents, and were therefore not only unpleasant and irksome but created disgust. Experience will convince us that it avails nothing to force the mind of a student upon subjects for which he has no capacity. Every one will reddily admit that there are great varieties and even

---

following subjects seem to have been prescribed for all arts students there: for freshmen, language, mathematics, logic, and rhetoric; for sophomores, Greek and Latin, mathematics, and geography; for juniors, logic and rhetoric, Greek and Latin, and natural philosophy; for seniors, moral philosophy (ethics), Latin, logic, and rhetoric.

contrasts in the geniuses of Individuals; and of course few will maintain that the same course of study should be assigned to such opposite capacities.

(To be continued)

November 21 [probably 1794].

On SUITABLE COURSES OF STUDY: II

In the opening sentence, a portion of which is missing, Tompkins deplores the assigning to one student of

. . . studies illy adapted to his capacities, whilst [another student] inferior in natural endowments to himself may suddenly outstrip him and obtain the appellation of a genius . . . because their tasks or studies are more congenial to the talents of the latter. This was expected in some degree [as] a matter of pretty general occurrence, namely, why [out of] the great number who pass thro' all the stages of what is termed a liberal education, so few become conspicuous for their knowledge or literary endowments. And perhaps it may with truth be observed, that in proportion to the judicious management, in this particular, of the direc[tion] of institutions of learning in the same ratio will those seminaries become respectable and useful. Hence a reason may be assigned, very different however

[48]

from what is generally noticed, why the Colleges in the other States have hitherto obtained a greater Celebrity and Fame than ours. In the eastern States I am informed, and credit the information, that they are not so rigid in exacting from all that mechanical rotine of study which is generally required. If a student has a taste, genius or inclination for any particular science, they cherish it by permitting him to pursue that science in preference to the rest; hence at the same time that they make him a thorough proficient in that science, they promote Industry and application; for, the science for which he has a genius, and in which he is therefore most likely to excel is that which he will pursue with the greatest eagerness and delight. I will not pretend to deny that many are apt to make this objection, that their studies are not such as they relish, merely to excuse their idleness or neglect. But I am persuaded that a skilful [assignment of subjects will arouse interest] in the pursuit of knowledge. Besides this, there are other things which are [calculated] to allure to application and improvement and to cause [pleasure] . . . or disgust. It therefore behoves patrons of learning [to be] assiduous to encourage everything [which] may operate as a stimulus or incitement to knowledge on the one hand and to discountenance and discourage on the other whatever may have a contrary tendency. And for this reason alone, I am convinced that Female education is not sufficiently regarded. No truth needs less reasoning to establish it than that the approbation of the Fair sex has a most extensive influence on the conduct of a young gentleman. Hence making the course of Female education more extensive might be attended with the highest benefits to society. If the ladies are partial to a man of Wisdom and solid abilities, each would earnestly wish to become such an one, in order to partake of that applause. If pedants are disesteemed by them and coxcombs who decorate their superficies only, are despised for their frivolous accomplishments and deformity, solid literary accomplishments for this very consideration would be substituted in their stead by the other sex. If therefore the effect of Education is to improve the Understanding, the more general and thorough the Education of the ladies is, the less respect, popularity or esteem will pedantry and fantastic ornaments obtain among ladies who have been well educated . . . that external accomplishments, generally assume a character exalted above those of the mind, is [un]worthy of the regard of those who wish to promote the cause of Literature and make men of good understanding and solid abilities esteemed and respected. I will not pretend to intimate that the arts of Music painting and dancing etc. are superficial and useless ornaments; but that these possessed alone without the more durable and dignified accomplishments of the mind may be productive of evil consequences in Society[;] that is[,] to promote a general taste for amusements pleasures and accomplishments that are fantastic and vicious, instead of cherishing sentiments of esteem and admiration for true abilities and solid learning, so interesting to the literary world and so calculated to introduce those amusements and pleasures which have always increased the fame and glory of nations.

November 28, 1794.

On PUBLICATION

IN THE PERUSAL of a public paper, not [long] since, my eye was caught by an advertisement intended to vindicate the author of a late publication from the imputation of plagiarism. This circumstance did not fail to recal to my mind a truth which I have often endeavoured to support, that he whose appetite for fame, has induced him to become an auth[ority] (on so important a science as law) at the age of about Twenty one years, has exposed himself to the censure of the world for ambition, vanity and an imperfection in Judgment; This calamity ever attends those who become authors, at an early period of life; they create enemies and jealous rivals who perpetually endeavour to diminish this reputation by proclaiming abroad the least blemishes or imperfections which they may be able to discover and perhaps circulate injurious and salacious reports greatly exaggerated. This is probably the reason why some of the most eminent writers have

[51]

forborne to publish their productions, untill they were considerably advanced in life and also perhaps to avoid another charge usually suggested on such occasions that they were constrained to publish by necessity.

Whatever reputation a young man's writings may have, yet an early publication of them [may lead to] disappointment. . . . But should he in more mature and deliberate years wish to change those opinions or sentiments which he may have made public, he will find his reputation to suffer by it. "Nescit vox missa reverti"[19] if he has previously declared his notions he can never recant without censure for fickleness. These difficulties may induce him to forbear the publication of writings in after life which would add much lustre to his name and prove highly beneficial to mankind. In short the works of a young man will always be suspected—either that he has adopted the thoughts of others as his own, or that he has not allowed enough of the "limae labor"[20] upon them to make them worthy of perusal or that he has not in conformity to the directions of an eminent author laid up his writings repeatedly to be considered until he had polished them and fully established himself in those sentiments which he would deliver in them.

December 3, 1794.

[19] Literally, a word (or voice) having been sent forth does not know how to return. A word spoken cannot be recalled.

[20] Literally, labor of the file. Polishing of a literary composition.

VALEDICTORY ORATION

Delivered May 6, 1795, at the Commencement of Columbia College in St. Paul's Chapel, Broadway and Vesey Street, New York City.

WHETHER we consider philosophy [or history the] best sources of ideas, they are both pleasurable and at the same time highly beneficial. The one ban[ishes from] the mind every mean and abject desire, and inspires to grandest and most sublime conceptions; whilst [the other] holds out to our view a mirror to direct our conduct, and regulate our pursuits. From these sources flow those pure streams of pleasure, which lose no[ne of] their relish by enjoyment, but acquire additional sweetness the oftener they are tasted. They instruct the young, and afford a rational entertainment to old age.

The portrait which the elegant historian draws of the magnanimity and virtue of antciente heroes and sages, produces a most happy influence. Emanations of the divine flame which animated their breasts are communicated to the bosom of the emulating youth and lead him to atchievements worthy of immortality. Elevating his mind, while he is transported by the impetuosity of his imagination, he fancies himself in the midst of those fields, where, by their valour, the celebrated heroes of antiquity signalized themselves and gained the fairest wreath of everlasting fame. With glowing rapture he listens to the delightful numbers of the poet, and traces the mellifluous stream which flowed from the lips of the orator. He then strives to copy and perform what he so warmly has admired; and filled with noble emulation . . . he often rises far beyond himself. It is the knowledge of men and [of] the works of nature . . . [that] dispels the clouds of ignorance . . . augments the flame of universal experience, inspires the most noble and exalted ideas of the power, wisdom and goodness of the creator, and leads the mind from nature's works to nature's God.

Nor does less utility and delight result from the pleasing task of cultivating and exercising the imagination. This is the most brilliant faculty of the soul; and for want of its improvement, the operations of the mind are frequently dull and inactive. But the flowery and enchanting path of literature gradually elevates the imagination, and unfolds to the view of its enraptured votary, the most enlarged and delightful prospects. "His active fancy travels beyond sense, and pictures things unseen."

> Whate'er adorns
> The princely dome, the column and the arch,
> The breathing marble, and the sculptur'd gold,
> His tuneful breast enjoys. For him the Spring
> Distils her dews, and from the silken gem
> Its lucid leaves unfolds. For him the hand
> Of Autumn tinges every fertile branch
> With blooming gold and blushes like the morn.
> Each passing hour sheds tribute from her wing.
> And still new beauties meet his lonely walk
> And loves unfelt attract him. Not a breeze
> Flies o'er the meadow; not a cloud imbibes

COLUMBIA COLLEGE IN 1790

The setting Sun's effulgence; not a strain
From all the tenants of the warbling shade
Ascends, but whence his bosom can partake
Fresh pleasures, unreproved.

But the duty assigned [to me now compels m]e to request the indulgence of a [few minutes] in turn to pay the just tribute of gratitude to the Regents and Trustees, and to our beloved and Esteemed Instructors.

ADDRESS TO THE REGENTS

To you, worthy and respected Regents,[21] has been committed the important trust of disseminating knowledge throughout our State. The numerous seminaries of learning that have been established, and the flourishing situation to which many of them, under your care and inspection, have arrived, affords a delightful subject of contemplation to everyone who rejoices in the felicity of his fellow citizens, and is a high eulogium

---

[21] A body organized in 1784 in accordance with legislation enacted during that year, creating the University of the State of New York. The Board of Regents consisted of leading state officials, such as the governor, the president of the senate, the speaker of the assembly, the mayor of the City of New York, and so forth, and other prominent citizens named in the Act of 1784. This body received extensive authority to found schools and colleges, confer degrees, and, in short, to direct educational policy throughout the state. In a supplementary act, 1787, Jonathan G. Tompkins, the father of Daniel D. Tompkins, became one of the regents—a position which he held for many years thereafter. Franklin B. Hough, *Historical and Statistical Record of the University of the State of N. Y.*, Albany, 1885, pp. 39 ff.

on your characters. Long will your names be recollected with gratitude—and as we have been allowed to taste the streams of knowledge, we return you our most unfeigned thanks. With an ardent desire that you may be successful in the glorious cause of diffusing knowledge throughout every part of the State; with the most anxious solicitude for your welfare, and our fervent prayers that you may receive, both here and hereafter, the high reward of good citizens and good men, we bid you farewell.

TO THE TRUSTEES

Honoured and respectable Trustees;[22] our favoured Columbia, of which we have the honour to be alumni, has been the immediate object of your care and attention. If to be solicitous for training up useful men and useful citizens; if to devote ourselves [*sic*] to so laudable a purpose as regulating [our conduct merit] praise, you deserve distinguished honour. May the smiles of Fortune prosper your endeavours, the voice of an approving conscience animate your exertions, and the warm expressions of our grateful hearts be accepted as the only tribute in our power to bestow.

---

[22] *Ibid.*, pp. 54-62. A body named and organized in 1787 under the act of April 13 noted immediately above. Provision was made for limiting the number of trustees to twenty-four, who were empowered to fill vacancies and to regulate generally the affairs of the college. In consequence of this act the Board of Regents was divested of direct control of the institution.

VALEDICTORY ORATION

MOST VENERABLE PRESIDENT

Permit us, this day, to make our public declaration of the affection we entertain for your character.[23] We esteem it the happiness of our lives that your usefulness has been extended to us; and we trust that the wise and pious instructions of your lips, has made impressions on our hearts, which the future occurrences of life shall neither obliterate nor destroy. When we carry our views back to the time when, in the courts of justice, you stood forth the champion of virtue and of truth; when the bar presented the richest of its treasures, and laid all its laurels at your feet—when admiring crowds stood mute with rapture, listening to the persuasive voice defending the rights of innocence—when again we see you called from the Forum to the councils of the state, from the state to the general government of our nation and here behold you respected and beloved; and then consider that for *us* you left the [sup]reme and applauding senate of our [nation] and returned . . . to direct us in the paths of science . . . what language can describe the feel-

---

[23] The first president of Columbia College, 1787-1800, was William Samuel Johnson (1727-1819), statesman, jurist, and educator; delegate to the Continental Congress; member of the Confederation Congress, 1784-87; delegate to the Constitutional Convention at Philadelphia, 1787; U. S. Senator from Connecticut. When the National Capital was transferred from New York City to Philadelphia, President Johnson resigned his seat in the Senate.

ings of our hearts or express our esteem, our veneration and our love? May you long continue the friend and father of the [Youth] and may the evening of your life be as peaceful and serene as the former part of it has been glorious.

TO THE PROFESSORS

I must next, my worthy Professors,[24] in the name of my fellow graduates, express to you the high sense we entertain of your characters and your worth. With **yo**u we have lived as pupils and as friends. We have listened with pleasure to your counsels; been improved by your example, and learned the ways of virtue and of truth. With us it now remains to practice what we know, and to improve those blessings we have enjoyed. We have experienced your assiduity and care in the line of your professions—we have known your unabated zeal to make us useful men, a blessing to our friends, and an ornament to our country. By you our faults have been reproved and our errors have been corrected—whilst those follies which are incident to youth and spring more from nature than from

---

[24] The following persons were members of the Faculty of Arts at Columbia while Tompkins was a student there: Elijah Dunham Rattoone, Professor of Greek and Latin; John Kemp, Professor of Mathematics and Geography; James Kent, Professor of Law; Samuel Latham Mitchill, "Professor of Natural History, Chemistry, Agriculture, and the other Arts depending thereon." *Catalogue of Columbia College,* New York, 1882, pp. 22-25.

choice, we have observed, have been always treated
with a kind and gentle hand; and the time has now
arrived when we must begin to see, and no doubt
shall be hereafter fully convinced, that severity and
discipline have resulted not from inclination, but
from . . . [affec]tion. Our own interest, and [the
interest of] society, have taught us that government
must be executed with firmness and decision as well
as with tenderness and care. Had this been otherwise,
you might have possessed our love, but not our respect. We might have considered you good men but
not as good teachers—we might have regarded you
in your private, but not in your public capacity. But,
our beloved and respected Professors, we must now
bid you adieu. We must now withdraw from your
guardianship, and cease to be protected by your care
—you may attend us with your prayers—you may
give us your blessing, but your constant presence,
your tender solicitude, your immediate counsel, and
advice, we must this day resign. But whither are we
going? Where must be our future destiny? What the
course and issue of our lives? Tomorrow's sun shall
rise and find us in a wide, and to us an unknown
world. We are unacquainted with its temptations;
we are ignorant of its snares. We have heard from
you, our faithful directors and our guides, that the
world is the grand theatre of action, where virtue is
to be tried—where discretion and prudence are con-
stantly requisite—where latent dangers perpetually

await us, and the arts of deception and guile present themselves on every side. With Providence for our guide, thither we bend our inexperienced course; and oh! may the attendant spirit of [Deity] and ye guardian angels whom we trust [forever] to watch around the young, preside over . . . our ways and direct us . . . And to you, our friends and professors, [the only recompense] we can make is the deepest sense of our obligation, the tenderest attachment to your happiness [and] fame, and our hearty prayers that you may long continue to be a blessing to this institution and to the world. May we, taught by your example as well as precept, strive to add virtue to our knowledge; that when this changing scene is ended, we may all meet where friends can never part and bliss can never end.

TO THE GRADUATES

My beloved classmates,[25] the events of this day must excite in our breasts emotions which can better be felt than expressed. "The memory of joys that are past, is pleasant and mournful to the soul." When we remember with what feeling and sentiment we have enjoyed our delightful hours,—with what reciprocal kindness and friendship our hearts have become knit together—how painful the reflection, that

---

[25] *Ibid.*, pp. 55-56. This graduating class consisted of twenty-five members, at least eight of whom became lawyers; nine, ministers; one, a merchant; one, a physician; and one, an army officer.

we must this day part, never, perhaps, to meet again!
On yonder smiling green, what mirth, what joy were
ours! never to be enjoyed again but in the flattering
illusions of fancy! "Precious moments! how swiftly
have they gone! Oh! commence again your delightful course! Flow on in remembrance, with longer
duration than you did in reality in your [first] suc-
cession." We are now about to enter into troublous
and complicated scenes of life. [In] the great theatre
of the world, we shall [play] our parts in [varied]
occupations. That we [may perform] the various
duties which will [involve] new situations and new
relations, let us embrace [virtue] and religion as our
rule and guide, and follow the directions of the great
philosopher of our country: "Let us be studious in
our professions, and we shall be learned; industrious, and we shall be opulent; temperate, and we
shall be healthy; let us be virtuous, and we shall be
happy."[26] Feelingly alive to all the impulses of
friendship, and deeply sensible of the numerous acts
of kindness I have received from you all, I feel a
regret, a sorrow for our separation which I cannot
express. May you all be distinguished and useful—
may you all be virtuous and happy—and, when in
your leisure moments, reflection transports you back

---

[26] Tompkins was apparently quoting from Benjamin Franklin. The exact quotation, from Franklin's essay on early mar-
riages, is as follows: "Be studious in your profession, and you
will be learned. Be industrious and frugal, and you will be
healthy. Be in general virtuous, and you will be happy."

to the late happy period of our lives, and revives all the tender scenes in the collegiate path, may you suffer the remembrance to dwell in your minds of a fellow student who now bids you all an affectionate and, perhaps, a long adieu.

TO THE STUDENTS

To you who have not yet completed your collegiate course, permit us to recommend in the language of friendship, diligence and perseverance in the pursuits of science. You are now laying the foundations of eminence and fame. Improve the precious moments . . . Your advantages are singular. . . . What college on the continent [is so well, or better, equipped] with the necessary means of instruction? [Where] will you find teachers who devote so great [an amount] of their time to the actual duties of their profession? With an excellent library at your command—with noble apparatus to display the works of nature and the science of philosophy—with lectures to unfold the wisdom of the antcients and the improvements of modern times— in yon fair temple of knowledge you may listen to the rhetorick of a Blair—learn the duties of justice, temperance and religion—soar aloft into the clouds and range amidst the planetary system, or descend into the Earth and view the causes and wonderful effects of things—there may you trace the classic page replete with knowledge, elegance and beauty—

catch the sublime spirit which fired the Moeonian bard, or be soothed with the soft numbers of the Mantuan swan. In short, whether Law, Divinity or Physic be your aim—whether Agriculture or Trade is to be made a science, there may you lay the foundation to advantage. Go on then students of Columbia, with eminence and glory in your view. In this land of liberty and peace, genius may extend her wings, unshackelled by the restraints of arbitrary power. And real fame, true and lasting honour, belong only to the virtuous and the good. . . . With tender wishes for your prosperity and happiness, we bid you . . . be virtuous! be happy.

I cannot conclude without returning my sincere thanks to this polite and brilliant audience for their kind attention this day. May the citizens of our Republic be ever persuaded that the interests of science are nearly connected with the liberty and happiness of their Country. General Knowledge must be the basis of our glory and independence; cherish, therefore, institutions of learning, as the ornaments and blessings of our land. Ye Patriots of America—ye patrons of science, may you long continue the friends and benefactors of mankind. And it is our most fervent wish, dictated by gratitude, that the smiles of beauty and the roses of health, may long continue to bloom on the cheeks of the fair daughters of New York.

INDEX

Addison, Joseph, "A Letter from Italy," in *Works of the English Poets from Chaucer to Cowper,* 18*n*

Africans, *see* Slaves

Alexander, DeAlva Stanwood, *Political History of the State of New York,* xiii*n*

American Scenic and Historic Preservation Society, *25th annual report* (1920), vii*n*

Argus (Albany), quoted, xii*n*

Arts, in America, 17

Authors, modern, *see* Modern authors

Authorship, 51 f.

Blair, Hugh, *Lectures on Rhetoric and Belles-Lettres,* 19 and note, 21, 62

Bolton, R., *History of Westchester County,* xii*n*

Books, reading of, 20

Campbell, Malcolm, preparatory school maintained by, xii

Capital punishment, 21 f., 22*n*, 23

City: advantages for study, 7; distractions of, 7

Classical education, advocated by Tompkins, x

Classical languages, 5 ff., 27

Classical poetry, disadvantages, 27 ff.

Classical prose, advantages, 27 ff.

Columbia College, xii; advantages of, 62; *Catalogue,* 1882, quoted, 58*n*; Class of 1795, 60 and note; course of study, 47; faculty of, 58 and note, 59; Latin and Greek requirements, 5*n*; president of, 57 and note; *Statutes of Columbia College, in New York,* "Plan of Education," 5*n*; students, 62 f.; trustees of, 56 and note

Composition, *see* English composition

Country life: advantages for poets, 41; distractions of, 7

Courses of study, 46 ff.

Daily Tribune (New York), quoted, xii*n*

Dead languages, *see* Classical languages

Dishonesty, 29 f.

Drunkenness, 9 ff., 23

Elections, safeguards of happiness and liberty, 2

[65]